RAPTORS FOSSILS FINS &FANGS

A PREHISTORIC CREATURE FEATURE

RAY TROLL & BRAD MATSEN

TRICYCLE PRESS
BERKELEY, CALIFORNIA

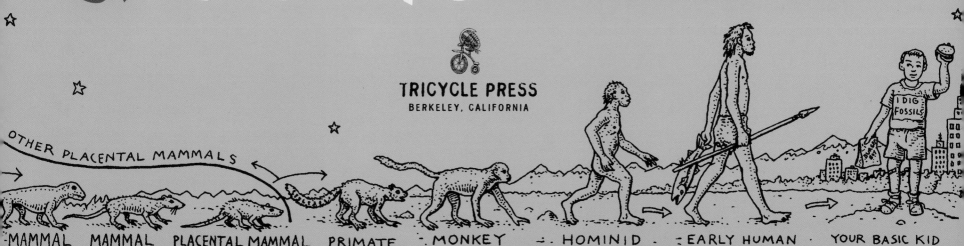

OTHER PLACENTAL MAMMALS

MAMMAL   MAMMAL   PLACENTAL MAMMAL   PRIMATE   · MONKEY   ·- HOMINID ·   - EARLY HUMAN ·   YOUR BASIC KID

I DIG FOSSILS

Cambrian Explosion

About 550 million birthdays ago, way before dinosaurs and people, the earliest relatives of all animals that you could easily see without a microscope appeared quite suddenly in the oceans of our planet. Life seemed to explode in just a few million years during the time we call the **Cambrian period**. Why then? Probably because the water and the air of earth finally contained enough oxygen to support complex animals. These swimming, squirming ancestors didn't look anything like you or a Tyrannosaurus to start with, of course. But some of the descendants of these weird and cool creatures changed through time to become first fish, then amphibians, reptiles, mammals, you, me, and every other animal. That kind of changing over time is called evolution. Strictly speaking, you are a fish. Yes, it's true. Stay tuned.

Trilobites

Paleontologists—the men and women who study fossils—have learned that, over time, it's the kinds of animals with hardy ancestors and plenty of good luck that survive. Others live for a while and then disappear. They become extinct. Though gone forever, these ancient animals often left clues that tell us the amazing story of life. Bones, shells, teeth, and tracks that were buried and protected from decay can turn into fossils. **Trilobites** (TRI-lo-bites) make especially great fossils because when they were alive they had hard shells made from minerals from the sea. Their name comes from the word "tri," which means three, and from their bodies, which had three parts, or lobes. Trilobites were animals without backbones. They were also the first animals with really good eyes. Trilobites were eating and being eaten in the ocean for almost 300 million years before becoming extinct.

Eurypterids Run the Show

A giant extinct sea scorpion called a **eurypterid** (You-RIP-terid) is a horror movie nightmare even as a fossil in a museum display case. But it gets really scary if you imagine you are a three-inch-long fish with no jaws and no shell being chased by a six-foot-long eurypterid. That's what was happening before our fishy ancestors got tough and fast. By the **Silurian period**, fish did have a cool new feature: a backbone. It helped them eat and fight and eventually win out over eurypterids and other bullies. Eurypterids were among the first living things to leave the sea. We know they came ashore because paleontologists have found fossils on land with traces of their tracks.

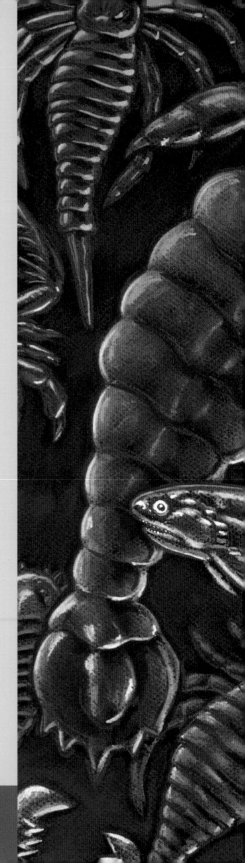

6

Fish out of Water

For a long time, fish had backbones but no jaws, so they could only suck their food. But by the **Devonian period**, fish evolved fins for swimming fast and chasing prey, and real jaws for snapping up a meal. Fish were in control, and the sea was full of slashing teeth, tails, and fins. The ocean environment was changing and land may have become the better place to live. From air sacs in their bodies, some fish developed lungs for breathing out of water. Finally, some, called lobefins, grew fins as strong as legs, and vertebrates were ready to leave the sea to try their luck on land. The Devonian was the only time, so far, that fish have come ashore and stayed long enough to evolve.

The Lucky Fish Gets the Cheeseburger

Just kidding about the cheeseburger. But our back-boned ancestors probably did leave the sea because they were looking for an easy meal. The land had already been invaded by plants and invertebrates from the sea, so there was plenty for the lobefin fish to eat. For a long time, not much was around to eat them. The best part of the story is that every single solitary land vertebrate ever since grew from those first lobefin fish which came ashore 375 million years ago. Yes, it's true. You are a fish. Your cats, dogs, and guinea pigs are fish. Einstein was a fish. Elvis was a fish. And your mom and dad are fish, too.

One Small Step for a Fish, One Giant Leap for Fishkind

Nobody knows exactly what kind of vertebrate was the first to live on land, but lobefins, legs, and life ashore are definitely connected. It might have been a kind of lobefin fish named **Panderichthys** (Pan-dur-IK-theez), like the one at the bottom of this picture. Panderichthys had strong fins with bones and muscle, almost like legs. They were good hunters, with fangs on the roofs of their mouths for grabbing slippery prey. Or maybe the first land pioneer was **Acanthostega** (Ah-kan-tho-STEG-a), an amphibian—a kind of animal that can live both on land and in water. Although it came from a lobefin fish, Acanthostega was the next step in the evolutionary line. Then many more millions of years brought reptiles, mammals, you and me. Whoever was first, in a few million years land vertebrates had actual legs and were thriving.

12

PERIOD:		SILURIAN	DEVONIAN	CARBONIFEROUS	PERMIAN	TRIASSIC	JURASSIC
MILLIONS OF YEARS AGO:		439	408	362	290	245	208	145

Bizarre Prehistoric Sharks

Like everything else on the planet, the fish that stayed in the sea kept right on changing. Sharks are among their most famous and scary relatives. The shapes of ancient sharks are hard for paleontologists to figure out because their skeletons were made of cartilage, the same kind of stuff that makes up most of your nose. Sharks don't leave very good fossils since cartilage, skin, and flesh rot. Usually, fossil hunters only find shark teeth and, if they're lucky, fossilized impressions of the cartilage. We have to guess a lot to imagine what they looked like. But we have enough clues from the shapes and positions of the fossils to know that sharks tried out some very bizarre bodies. For instance, look at the **Iniopterygians** (In-ee-op-ter-IJ-ee-uns) at the top of this picture. Iniops had funny, finny wings on their backs and probably flapped like birds through the water.

PERIOD:		DEVONIAN	CARBONIFEROUS	PERMIAN	TRIASSIC	JURASSIC
MILLIONS OF YEARS AGO:		408	362	290	245	208	145

"MISTER ED"

EDESTUS GIGANTEUS

Scissor Tooth and Buzzsaw Sharks

Some of the terrible, fierce sharks of long ago didn't need the Tooth Fairy. Instead of shedding their teeth as they grew bigger, **Helicoprion** sharks (Hel-i-ko-PRI-un) kept them in their jaws in weird whorls like buzz saws. **Edestus giganteus** (Ee-DEST-oos gi-GAN-te-us) shed some teeth and kept the rest in two rows like scissor blades. Modern sharks have many rows of teeth and constantly shed them. Prehistoric sharks, though, were still sorting through the many possible kinds of jaws and teeth, and this was the best and meanest they could do. Compared to Helicoprion and Ed the Shred, a Great White Shark could be in a petting zoo.

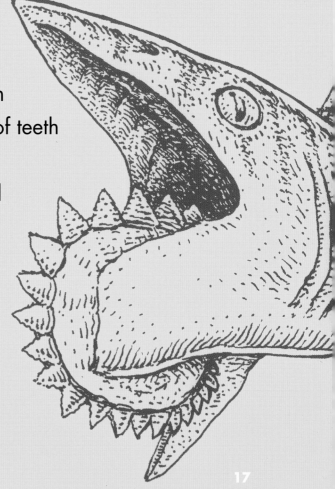

17

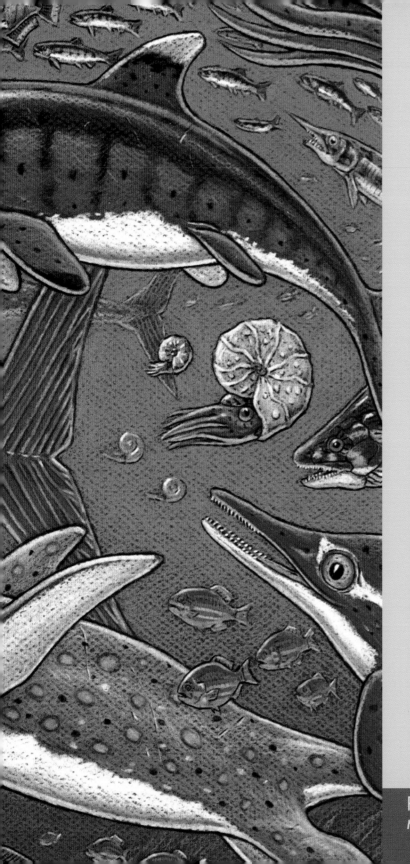

Jurassic Sea

By the time the dinosaurs were stomping around on land, the ocean was full of snarling, snapping, hungry life. Fish and sharks were everywhere, of course, some of them bigger than any before or since. Schools of squid and **ammonites** (AM-on-ites) as big as merry-go-rounds glided through the murky depths. Even some reptiles had left the land and returned to the sea to become real sea monsters. **Ichthyosaurs** (IK-thee-o-sores) look a lot like modern dolphins except they were reptiles, not mammals. Their tails pointed up and down instead of side to side. **Plesiosaurs** (PLEASE-ee-o-sores) were the spitting image of the famous-but-not-real Loch Ness monster. All the giant marine reptiles disappeared with the dinosaurs and no one knows for sure why or how.

19

PERIOD:	PERMIAN	TRIASSIC	JURASSIC	CRETACEOUS
MILLIONS OF YEARS AGO:	290	245	208	145	65

Bigger Than a House

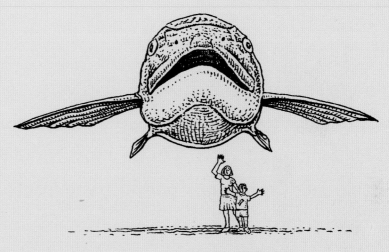

An English farmer and fossil hunter who lived near the city of Leeds found the first parts of this biggest-of-all fish. From the size of the bits of fin and bone, paleontologists think **Leedsichthys** (Leeds-IK-theez) would have been between 60 and 100 feet long—much bigger than your house. Get a big net before you fish for this one.

Actually, you can't catch a Leedsichthys or see Ed the Shred in your city's aquarium because the earth goes through violent changes every few million years or so. Weird ancient fish, bizarre prehistoric sharks, and most of the animals that have ever lived, are extinct. Huge numbers of animals die all at once during mass extinctions, possibly caused by changes in climate, disease, giant volcanic eruptions, or even meteors from space. Some critters are strong and lucky and their descendants continue the voyage of life.

Good Gracious, Cretaceous

The earth's surface is always moving very, very slowly, so that over millions of years the ocean and land change places. The best fossils of the amazing late **Cretaceous period** come from Kansas and the middle of what is now North America because that's where part of the ocean was way back then. Just before the dinosaurs and lots of other land creatures disappeared, the oceans teemed with turtles, fish, giant reptiles, and big swimming birds. The skies, too, were alive with flying reptiles called **Pterosaurs** (TER-a-saurs), some as big as jet fighters.

Rip, Snap, Slurp

Meanwhile, back on land, the other sons and daughters of those fabulous lobefin fish were the stars of the show: dinosaurs. For a long time, paleontologists thought they were slow and dumb, but newly discovered fossils and changing scientific thinking tell us that some dinosaurs were fast, hot blooded, and pretty smart. Toothy meat-eaters like **Tyrannosaurus** (Ty-RAN-a-sore-us) and **Deinonychus** (Dine-on-EYE-kus) were ferocious predators. Deinonychus was part of a nasty group of dinosaurs called **raptors**. They were swift, agile, and had huge, ripping claws on their middle toes which they used to slash the bellies of their prey. They ran around on their hind legs, like the birds in your yard to which they are related. (Think about *that* family tree next time you eat turkey for dinner.)

Raptors, Gators & Gars

Gars are a kind of long, snake-like fish that live in rivers in the midwestern and southern United States even now. They have scary jaws full of needle-sharp teeth, their scales are like armor, and they can breathe air as well as take oxygen from the water. But the coolest thing about them is that gars just like them were alive at the same time as the dinosaurs. Fish like the gars, reptiles like the alligators, mammals, and many other vertebrates survived the mass extinction that killed off the large dinosaurs. Lots of aquariums have tanks of gars, and it's fun to imagine those tough, patient fish watching from the water while a pack of raptors prowls the river bank.

PERIOD:	CARBONIFEROUS	PERMIAN	TRIASSIC	JURASSIC	CRETACEOUS	TERTIARY	QUATERNARY
MILLIONS OF YEARS AGO:	362	290	245	208	145	65	1.64 · NOW!

Sabertooth Salmon

Fangs have been part of the evolution of many animals, like cats and warthogs. Some fish grew fangs to help them eat and fight for survival. And about 12 million years ago, some salmon were great fanged beasts ten feet long weighing 500 pounds. The **sabertooth salmon** are related to modern salmon, but don't worry about an attack next time you go swimming. Like so many of the way-cool creatures of long ago, they are extinct. But that's life.

PERIOD:	PERMIAN	TRIASSIC	JURASSIC	CRETACEOUS	TERTIARY	QUATERNARY
MILLIONS OF YEARS AGO:	290	245	208	145	65	1.64 NOW!

Looking Back, Looking Forward

Fish still swim in the sea, changing steadily into who-knows-what, while we and the other descendants of the lobefin fish that came ashore wait for what is next here on land. What will the lobefins' descendants look like in millions of years? Will they be around at all? Will anything you'd recognize as human still be around? Or will you and your neighbors have gone the way of the raptors? Of course, nobody knows, but the real fun is in watching the amazing story of life unfold, not in knowing the ending. The first fish that came ashore all those many years ago could not have known what its great, great, great-times-a-gazillion grandkid—that's you—would look like.

PERIOD:	PERMIAN	TRIASSIC	JURASSIC	CRETACEOUS	TERTIARY	QUATERNARY	
MILLIONS OF YEARS AGO:	290	245	208	145	65	1.64	NOW!

For Corinna and Patrick—R.T.

For Laara, Henry, and Sam—B.C.M.

For Michelle—K.T.

Evolution is a process that can take millions of years. Some of the creatures in these paintings may not have been contemporaries. For more information, read Planet Ocean by Ray Troll and Brad Matsen, published by Ten Speed Press, and available at bookstores or by calling 1-800-841-BOOK.

The color illustrations were created with pastels, the line drawings with pen and ink. In reality, the creatures featured may not have been the same colors Ray Troll imagined.

Text copyright © 1996 by Brad Matsen and Ray Troll
Illustrations copyright © 1996 by Ray Troll
Book design by Kate Thompson

Tricycle Press
P.O. Box 7123
Berkeley, California 94707

Library of Congress Cataloging-in-Publication Data
Troll, Ray 1954–
    Raptors, fossils, fins & fangs : a prehistoric creature feature /
Ray Troll & Brad Matsen.
        p. cm.
    Includes index.
    Summary: Introduces lesser known prehistoric creatures, including the giant sea scorpion called a eurypterid, the helicoprion shark, and the carniverous land dinosaur Deinonychus.
        ISBN 1-883672-41-4 Casebound / ISBN 1-883672-75-9 Paperback
        1. Animals, Fossil—Juvenile literature. [1. Prehistoric animals.]   I. Matsen, Bradford.   II. Title.
QE765.T76   1996
560—dc20   96—1823
                                                                                        CIP
                                                                                        AC

First Tricycle Press printing, 1996
First paperback printing, 1998
Manufactured in Hong Kong
2 3 4 5 6 — 02 01 00